# Chocolate or Vanilla?
## Choosing Freedom in Christ
## Second Edition

Anita Dillard
16128 Meadow St.
Romulus, MI 48174

## Dr. Robert Retherford

## Dr. Katherine Scranton

## Printed in the United States of America

Dr. Robert Retherford & Dr. Katherine Scranton

# <u>CONTENTS</u>

# FOREWORD

Authentic healing begins with a relationship, first and foremost with God. Dealing with our emotions is part of having that relationship. Dr. Robert Retherford provides us with tools to truly get in touch with our wounded "selves" and the negative emotions set aside and ignored for most of our lives. God has given him awesome revelation into this unique area of inner healing. He provokes us to "feel and deal" with our woundedness. He proves there is no shortcut to healing. If not dealt with, he substantiates the consequences through the ways people demonstrate their woundedness, including in most forms of addiction. He is a very compassionate and patient person, and the many testimonies found in this book validate his approach. It should be read and applied by all of us; we all need healing in our lives. By the way, Dr. Bob, I choose vanilla, and I choose it just because I do!

Drs. Jerry & Sherill Piscopo
Evangel Association of Churches and Ministries

# PREFACE

In reading this book, you will find a road map to emotional healing that is entirely biblical. My goal is to provide the steps you need to follow to find your freedom in Christ so that you can walk in God's love and be free from the emotional bondage that has kept you from experiencing the peace, joy, and love God desires for you to have.

I have been counseling as a licensed counselor for forty-one years. I am also a licensed minister. Throughout my years of counseling, I have been a devout Christian and have received the revelations I describe within these pages. It is my hope and prayer that everyone who reads these pages receives the full revelation of my teaching. For most people, I believe that once they understand these teachings, they can begin to apply them and see major life changes within a matter of weeks. Healing is a lifelong journey, but keys to understanding the Word of God can shorten the process, as God uses different tools to help us to go free. As we walk through our healing process He will establish us in our position in the body of Christ, where we can serve out of love and freely share God's love and revelation with others.

The book talks a lot about positional righteousness – that righteousness imputed to us by God and made possible through our position in Christ. Even though we have positional righteousness, God still expects us to repent and turn from our sins. The intended purose of the book is to help those who have turned from their sins to the best of their ability, but continue to struggle to get the victory in some areas of their life.

Throughout the book I have included real-life examples from my ministry. Details such as names and genders have been changed to protect the identity of my clients. This book belongs to God. He alone can heal and this book simply summarizes some of what He has already explained in the books of the Bible.

Dr. Robert A. Retherford
Member of the EACM

Dr. Robert Retherford & Dr. Katherine Scranton

# CHAPTER 1

# <u>IDENTIFYING THE PROBLEM</u>

*▱*

Elaine came to me completely frustrated by a child she had recently adopted. The child was headstrong and stubborn, but Elaine was hesitant to be too strict because the child had already threatened to run away when previously punished. Elain was resentful and angry with her daughter. Being angry at her was a subtle way of blaming the child, and yelling did not do anything to solve the problem. The Apostle Paul says, "Fathers do not exasperate your children; instead, bring them up in the training and instruction of the Lord."[1] He also says not to "war against flesh and blood,"[2] which was what Elaine was doing when she made her daughter the problem instead of looking at her own negative thoughts and beliefs.

During our subsequent sessions, we dug into Elaine's thoughts and feelings. It turned out that she was very insecure about raising children. She felt incompetent and feared being a bad mother. The bottom line and the real "problem" was her insecurity. Once we were able to identify her problem and work through her emotions and negative beliefs, she was able to change her belief system about herself. Now Elaine has no problem disciplining her daughter appropriately, and the child responds well. In fact, Elaine now has two adopted children, and both are well behaved and flourishing.

Over the course of my forty-one years of practice, I have had many different "problems" presented to me by my clients. As in Elaine's story, the problem that is usually presented to me during the first session is not really the problem at all. The problem is not our trials and tribulations from the past; the problem is not our parents, our children, our spouses, the things we have done, or the things that have happened to us. The problem is almost always our false belief system. We tend to believe the lies about who we are in our sin nature when we should believe the truth about who we are in Christ. By making anything other than our belief system the problem, we are avoiding the root of what we need to deal with to be free in Christ.

Wrong beliefs can keep us rooted in our old, sinful ways. The Bible says, "For as he thinketh in his heart, so is he."[3] In other words, we are what we think. We need to overcome our thoughts and beliefs that don't line up with God's Word. Until we deal with our lie-based beliefs we will struggle with outward sin as well. We can modify our behavior but there will be no lasting change without a change in our belief systems.

Elaine believed she was not an adequate parent, but that is not what Jesus would say about her. Jesus would say that she could discipline her child in a godly manner, and be successful at parenting, if she could come into agreement with God about who she is in Him. Elaine believed she was insecure and incompetent as a mother. In Christ she is secure and competent to do all things that He has called her to do.

Elaine needed to recognize what she believed about herself in her sinful nature and rid herself of the emotions attached to her flawed belief system. She could then change her mind to believe what God says about her now that she is saved. In the Spirit she walks in love, just as God is love. Part of loving our children is disciplining them when necessary. By walking in the Spirit of God, she can discipline her children out of God's love, even as God disciplines us from time to time.[4] I met with Elaine again at a later date and asked her how things were going for her and her children. She explained, "It's very simple. I make the rules, and they follow them." I also spoke to her daughter. When I asked her whether she was going to go to the movies that day she told me, "I don't know. I'll have to ask my mom. She's the boss."

## The Transformation

We are born into sin, and we are controlled by it when we are walking in the sin nature. We are all born with a sinful nature, and as a result we experience a low self-image with thoughts of inadequacy, unworthiness, and not being good enough. Our problem is the way we think. God says, "For my thoughts are not your thoughts, neither are your ways my ways."[5] Paul said, "I do not do the good I want to do, but the evil I do not want to do—this I keep on doing."[6] Why? Because of the sin that lies within him.

When we are saved we are immediately made righteous in Christ. Everything changes! We become who the Bible says we are. In Christ, we are righteous, holy, and pure because Jesus died as a sacrifice for our sins. Our sins are now covered with His blood.

As we learn who we are in Christ, we begin to exhibit what the Bible calls "the fruit of the Spirit." "The fruit of the Spirit is love, joy, peace, forbearance, kindness, goodness, faithfulness, gentleness and self-control."[7] All this fruit will be present when we walk in the Spirit, and when we love, we fulfill all the commandments. Jesus's sacrifice for us frees us from sin and the law of sin; and allows us to live as Jesus did, being effective in our good deeds and in our walk with God.

When we accept Christ, and begin to learn more about God's laws, we begin to see the magnitude of our sin relative to God's holiness. This can become death to us without revelation regarding His grace. We must understand that we are no longer under the old law, but through salvation, we have a new covenant based on God's grace. Without this understanding, along with the comfort and teaching of the Holy Spirit, we can easily begin to condemn (blame) others and ourselves. This is not what God desires.[8] Rather we must deal head-on with our false beliefs so that we can change our minds and accept who we are in Christ. Remember, we are what we think we are. As we deal with our false beliefs, our actions will begin to line up with the Word of God.

> *Therefore, there is now no condemnation for those who are in Christ Jesus.*
>
> -Romans 8:1

Being aware of our sin without knowing that God sees the good in us can cause us to spiral into greater sin. This is why the Bible teaches us about the new covenant and stresses the importance of God's love, forgiveness and mercy. Most addictions are birthed from our desire to avoid the reality of our sins and to medicate our emotional pain. Being more aware of our sin can actually make us feel worse, which may lead us to sin more! This is where we need to learn to take responsibility for our sin without condemning ourselves or beating up on ourselves. Sin is something that every human being faces, so there is no need to condemn ourselves; we simply need to accept it for what it is. We need to accept our sin and still understand who we are in Christ. The Bible says that we are righteous and holy regardless of our outward behavior.

## The Good News

Paul summarizes the good news of Jesus Christ in his letter to the church in Colosse. He says, "Once you were alienated from God and were **enemies in your minds** because of your evil behavior. But now he has reconciled you by Christ's physical body through death to present you **holy in His sight, without blemish and free from accusation—if you continue in your faith,** established and firm, not moved from the hope held out in the gospel"[9]

There are some key points we can take from Paul's brief description of the good news of Jesus

Christ. Please note that we were enemies "in our minds" toward God prior to Christ's sacrifice for our sins on the cross. It is in our minds that the trouble begins. The good news is we have been reconciled to God, and we are now "holy in His sight." God actually sees us as being without sin because Jesus died so that our sins would be forgiven and even forgotten. We are washed clean. God says we **are** holy! He doesn't say that we are becoming holy. **He says that we already are holy!**

God sees the good in us! In this book we will talk about changing our belief systems and mindsets to be in line with the way God sees us. It is crucial to recognize that the only reason we have been changed and can change our minds and find our freedom is because of Christ. He has made us holy through His blood. We can never become holy though our behavior. We will never be good enough. The Bible says our righteousness is like filthy rags.[10] Try as we may to be holy, apart from the blood of Jesus our efforts are futile. Even if we did attain some level of righteousness apart from God, it would be as filthy rags before the Lord. We will never be good enough to stand in the presence of God. The good news is, we are holy through Christ's blood, and because of His blood we can enter the presence of God.

> *You were taught, with regard to your former way of life, to put off your old self, which is being corrupted by its deceitful desires; to be made new in the attitude of your minds; and to put on the new self, created to be like God in true righteousness and holiness.*
>
> -Ephesians 4:22-24

The Bible also says that we are made blameless if we "continue in our faith." Being blameless before God has nothing to do with our actions in our past, present, or future. Being blameless before God is based on His grace, our faith in Jesus Christ, and the knowledge that we have been transformed through His death, burial, and resurrection.

At the same time, it is obvious to us that our sin does not vanish upon salvation. We still need to go through a sanctification process to "put off" the old man and "put on" the new man. [11] Sanctification is the process of becoming more holy. To be sanctified, we must repent and turn from our sins to the best of our ability. Putting off the old man involves repentance. Then we must begin to align our beliefs with God's truth. This alignment is what needs to happen for us to "put on" the new man. The new man is who we are when we are walking in the Spirit. For example, God says we are worthy of His blessings and promises, but we may believe that we are unworthy. We can change our minds to believe that we are worthy and be set free from this misconception, but we must always remember

> *God made him who had no sin to be sin for us, so that in him we might become the righteousness of God.*
>
> **-2 Corinthians 5:21**

that it is only through Christ that we have become worthy. We are not worthy through anything we do. If our worthiness were based on our behavior, we could lose our worthiness at any time. God says we are worthy, and God is not a liar! As you read the chapters of this book, please keep in mind that it is only through Christ that we have become whole and have been set free. It has nothing to do with us, our performance, or our circumstances. God tells us who we are according to His Word and our identity is based on the shed blood of Jesus Christ. <u>Once you are saved</u> **<u>you become the righteousness of God in Christ.</u>** [12] The main purpose of this book is to help you change your mind from believing you are a sinner to believing you are righteous in Christ. Along with believing you are righteous, you can change your mind and accept all the privileges that go along with being righteous. Because of Him, once saved, you are righteous regardless of what the circumstances may suggest. Because you are in Christ you can decree the following facts about yourself:

I am -

God's child (John 1:12)
Forgiven (Eph. 1:7)
A new creation (2 Cor. 5:17)
A temple of the Holy Spirit (1 Cor. 6:19)
Delivered from the power of darkness (Col. 1:13)
Blessed (Gal. 3:9)

Holy and without blame (1 Pet. 1:16)
Victorious (Rev. 21:7)
Set free (John 8:31-33)
Strong in the Lord (Eph. 6:10)
More than a conqueror (Rom 8:37)
In Christ (1 Cor. 1:30)
Accepted in the beloved (Rom. 15:7)
Complete in Him (Col. 2:10)
Free from condemnation (Rom 8:1)
Reconciled to God (2 Cor. 5:18)
In the world as He is in heaven (1 John 4:17)
Overtaken with blessings (Eph. 1:3)
The righteousness of God (2 Cor. 5:21)
Called of God (2 Tim. 1:9-11)
Chosen (1 Pet. 2:5)
Healed by the stripes of Jesus (1 Pet. 2:24)
Seated in heavenly places (Eph. 2:6)
Beloved of God (Col. 3:12)

Yes, it's true that God expects us to change and put our sinful lives behind us. The Bible says, "Do not conform to the pattern of this world, but be transformed by the renewing of your mind. Then you will be able to test and approve what God's will is – his good, pleasing and perfect will."[13] This scripture indicates that if we are not renewed in our minds, we will not be transformed. As a result, we will likely conform to the pattern of the world – namely, sin.

This scripture helps us to understand how important it is to lay hold of God's truth about who we are. We will be transformed as we deal with our false beliefs. When we believe we are holy and righteous, we will begin to act holy and righteous. When we come into a closer relationship with God, we will stop sinning because we no longer want to sin. This book provides some practical steps to help you deal with your false beliefs, renew your mind and be transformed.

## **Endnotes**

[1] Eph. 6:4

[2] Eph. 6:12

[3] Prov. 23:7, KJV

[4] Heb. 12:11

[5] Isa 55:8

[6] Rom. 7:19

[7] Gal 5:22-23

[8] Rom. 8:1

[9] Col. 1:22-23a, emphasis added

[10] Isa. 64:6

[11] Eph. 4:22-24

[12] 2 Cor. 5:21

[13] Rom. 12:2

# CHAPTER 2

# <u>RELEASING THE SINS OF OTHERS</u>

This chapter provides information from the Bible that will help you to understand why we should release our sins and the sins of others to God and focus on dealing with our negative beliefs. The Bible is very clear when it says, "But if you do not forgive others their sins, your father will not forgive your sins."[1] You can see how important forgiveness is! It is in our best interest to choose to forgive.

From a practical standpoint, fighting with others about their sin has very little potential to help the situation. We must focus strictly on changing our false beliefs and pray for others rather than argue with them.

Approaching in love someone with whom you are having a disagreement is much more productive than reacting out of anger or yelling at the person out of hurt. Focusing on dealing with our false beliefs, rather than on a person's sins allows us to love those who have offended us. Those whom we are in conflict with will be much more receptive to our words if they are spoken calmly, rationally, and from a position of love.

## Separating Sin from Man

Adam and Eve bore many children, but the first of their offspring were Cain and Abel. The Lord rejected an offering that Cain had brought Him while accepting the offering from Cain's brother. As a result, jealousy rose up in Cain, and he decided to kill Abel.

> *As it is, it is no longer I myself who do it, but it is sin living in me. For I know that good itself does not dwell in me, that is, in my sinful nature. For I have the desire to do what is good, but I cannot carry it out.*
>
> -Romans 7:17-18

God, knowing Cain's thoughts, said, "But if you do not do what is right, **sin** is crouching at your door; **it** desires to have you but you must master **it**."[2] By stating it this way, God treats sin as a separate entity from man. Paul also speaks of sin as a separate entity from man throughout the book of Romans. For example, Paul says, "As it is, **it is no longer I who do it, but the sin living in me.** I know that nothing good lives in me, that is, in my sinful nature."[3] James and Peter speak of sin in a similar fashion in their letters. The important principle to note is they all separate man from his sin.

In separating someone from his or her sin, we can begin to accept the person without judging him or her. That is not to say people are not accountable for their sin, but separating the person from their sin allows us to love the person even while we dislike the sin that has been committed. In doing this we can give the sin to God in prayer and forgive the person, recognizing he or she is a human being who sins, as we do.

We can also give our own sin to God, believing His Word about repentance and how we can be free from sin, if we deal with our false beliefs. We can take responsibility for our sin, understanding that it's our thoughts that need to change. In doing this we can choose to release ourselves from self-condemnation.

When we can separate another person from his or her sin, we can give the trespass to God. That person might suffer before God on Judgment Day, and he or she is likely to suffer consequences on this earth as well. The person's consequences are not our concern. By giving the sin to God, we can trust the Lord to deal with it as He sees fit. We don't need to carry that burden anymore. We can trust Him with whatever judgment is due.

**Defining Who We Are**

Another important point is that by separating the sin nature from the person, we do not define the person — or ourselves — by the sin. God's Word defines who we are. If we can see the person, and ourselves, through the

> The voice spoke to him a second time, "Do not call anything impure that God has made clean."
>
> -Acts 10:15

28

eyes of God and by the Word of God, we are less likely to be condemning or judgmental. After all, who are we to call someone unclean that He has called clean?[4] In Romans, Paul says, "Who will bring any charge against those whom God has chosen? It is God who justifies."[5]

The Pharisees did the opposite of what God (and Paul) did. They identified men as "sinners," as if the sin defined the man. They labeled people as "sinners," as if they themselves had not sinned. The Pharisees asked Jesus, "Why do you eat and drink with tax collectors and 'sinners'?"[6] Jesus responded, "It is not the healthy who need a doctor but the sick. I have not come to call the righteous, but sinners to repentance."[7] Jesus was not saying that the Pharisees were not sinners; He was saying that until they **recognized** that they were sinners, they could not be helped. We can take responsibility for our sin without allowing it to define who we are. We are saints who sin. We are the righteousness of God. [8]

## Showing Mercy

One of the first things that must happen in our healing walks is that we must forgive others and ourselves. In fact, the Bible says that if we do not forgive others, then God will not forgive us.

*John's Testimony*

*When I was a child I thought that my father wanted to kill me. I lived in constant fear. My father's sin was difficult to forgive and give to the Lord. In fact, I held onto it for quite a long time, allowing bitterness and resentment to fester in my own soul.*

*I hated him and held tremendous unforgiveness toward him. During my healing journey, I realized that I was as much a sinner as he was. God says that if we have broken one of the commandments, we have broken them all. I certainly had transgressed God's law through my hateful thoughts.*

*The revelation that I was as sinful as my father was extremely hard for me to accept, but once I did so, it changed my entire worldview. Now I could see people through the eyes of God and knew they were righteous, or had the potential to be righteous, through the blood of Jesus.*

In our sinful nature, we are all essentially the same. We are sinners in need of a savior. When we recognize this, we can show mercy to others. The Pharisees couldn't show mercy, because they thought they were better than the "sinners." They neglected justice and mercy.[9]

Now that John sees his father through God's eyes as being very much the same as he in his sinful nature, he has empathy for his father. Anytime we put ourselves above someone else we pridefully judge that person's sin and heart. We cannot elevate ourselves to a higher position than someone else without becoming judgmental toward that individual.[10] Only God can judge a person's heart because only God knows the entire circumstance.

It is crucial to understand that we all sin if we are going to offer true forgiveness, mercy, and love. The Pharisees couldn't show mercy and sat in judgment of all men because they thought they were better than the "sinners." A parable that Jesus told in the Gospel of Luke paints a complete picture. Jesus said, "Two men went up to the temple to pray, one a Pharisee and the other a tax collector. The Pharisee stood up and prayed about himself: "God, I thank you that **I am not like other people**—robbers, evildoers, adulterers— or even like this tax collector.'"[11] Notice that the Pharisee said, **"I am not like other people."** We cannot have this attitude. If a person sins against us, we should step back and remind ourselves that this person sins

> It is because of him that you are in Christ Jesus, who has become for us wisdom from God—that is, our righteousness, holiness and redemption. Therefore, as it is written: "Let the one who boasts boast in the Lord."
>
> -1 Corinthians 1:30-31

just as we do. We need to give the sin to God and love the person right where he or she is. This is forgiving quickly, as we are called to do.

We should consider how we regard ourselves. Are we just as sinful as everyone else? If we think we have a unique or special capacity to be obedient, remember there is nothing we have that God did not give us,

"For who makes you different from anyone else? What do you have that you did not receive? And if you did receive it, why do you boast as though you did not?"[12] We need to fully understand that we simply "are." If we have special gifts of obedience, compassion, or mercy, God has blessed us. Others who seem to struggle may not have the gifts that we have.

## Choosing to Forgive

One practical step toward forgiveness is to make the choice to forgive. Forgiveness is not an emotion but your emotions will begin to be healed if you choose to forgive. John had tremendous unforgiveness toward his father. We can certainly understand why he had unforgiveness because he believed that his father wanted to kill him. First, John had to decide whether he was willing to forgive. Remember, God forgave him for his sins, and John should be willing to extend the same grace to his father.

Once you have made the choice to forgive, you should make a declaration out loud - for example, "I choose to forgive my father." By saying it out loud, you are notifying all the powers of darkness of your choice. You are making a public declaration that God will honor. Once you say you forgive out loud you should feel a release in your emotions. In time, God will honor your choice to be obedient and he will heal what remains of your bitterness and resentment.

Another practical step you can take toward your healing is to pray for those who have hurt or offended you. The Bible says to bless those who persecute you.[13] As you pray for them you will feel your heart begin to change toward them. You may even begin to feel empathy for them. I had a client who had been molested by her mother. As she began to pray for her mother, she began to realize how sick her mother was. She began to develop empathy toward her mother and she began to pray for her salvation. She found herself weeping and travailing for the salvation of her mother. In the process, God healed her of her unforgiveness, bitterness, and resentment. When we are obedient to God's Word, we will see great results in our own personal growth and healing.

## Endnotes

[1] Matt. 6:15

[2] Gen. 4:7, emphasis added

[3] Rom. 7:17-18, emphasis added

[4] Acts 10:15

[5] Rom. 8:33

[6] Mat. 9:11

[7] Mat. 9:12-13

[8] 2 Cor. 5:21

[9] Mat. 23:23

[10] 1 Cor. 1:30-31

[11] Luke 18:10-11, emphasis added

[12] 1 Cor. 4:7

[13] Rom. 12:14

# CHAPTER 3

# CHOCOLATE OR VANILLA

I once had a client whose husband had left her for someone else. They had not divorced, but he was traveling around to different states with another woman. Certainly, this client had a lot she could blame her husband for, but to receive her healing, she had to separate herself from his sin. Realizing there was nothing she could do about her husband's sin, she chose to work on dealing with **her own false beliefs** and change her thoughts and feelings about her circumstances.

Through our work together, she was able to deal with her anger, unforgiveness, and hurt. In doing this she was able to lay down her false beliefs, change her mindset, and begin to walk in the love of Christ. Her faith that her husband would return never wavered, and her communication with him now came from a much more loving perspective. Her loving attitude surprised her husband, given his horrible behavior. Eventually, he did come to counseling and focused on **his** false beliefs. As a result, they were able to work through their marital problems, and his wife has since written and published a book about her experiences.

## Chocolate or Vanilla                    # 4

To go free in Christ, we must first take responsibility for our feelings. It's difficult for us to take responsibility for our feelings, as we almost unknowingly blame others, situations, and events for who we believe we are. Just listen to the types of things we say: "You *make* me angry," or "*You* hurt me." This type of language gives power to others and removes our responsibility. If these statements were true, others would have to change before we could be healed. No one can **make** you feel or think a certain way. You are the only one you can do anything about.

*Shelly's Testimony*

*The day I met Dr. Retherford was a day I will never forget. Before we had even discussed much of anything he started asking me to choose between chocolate and vanilla ice cream. I thought to myself, "OK, this is a little strange." The chocolate or vanilla thing seemed like a game to me and made me laugh to myself, but I found out it was profound and central to his teaching.*

*Dr. Retherford continued to ask me to pick between the two ice creams. He explained to me that* **choices can have no reasons.** *He would say that decisions have reasons but for this exercise and for the purpose of his teaching,* **choices can have no reasons. To go free in Christ, you have to come to a place where you can make a choice without a reason. This is the only way you will be able to choose to believe the truth in the Word of God despite the circumstances in the present and the past.**

*The dialogue went something like this:*

*Dr. Retherford: Choose an ice cream based on what I told you about choices. For the purposes of our healing work,* **choices have no reasons.**

*Shelly: Chocolate.*

*Dr. Retherford: Why did you choose chocolate?*

*Shelly: Because I like chocolate.*

*Dr. Retherford: You just gave me a reason.* **Choices have no reasons.** *Choose an ice cream.*

*Shelly: Chocolate.*

*Dr. Retherford: Why did you choose chocolate?*

*Shelly: Because I prefer chocolate?*

*Dr. Retherford: You gave me a reason again. Preferring chocolate is a reason for your choice. Repeat after me. "Why did you choose chocolate?" But change the word "why" to "because."*

*Shelly: Because I chose chocolate.*

*Then Dr. Retherford asked me another question: Have you ever been hurt?*

*Shelly: Yes, all the time.*

*Dr. Retherford: Why are you hurt?*

*Shelly:* **Because I am hurt.**

*Dr. Retherford: And who have you been blaming?*

*Shelly: Everyone*

*The message had an impact on me. At first I was a little confused, but I realized he was saying that I am responsible for my feelings. I was hurt because* **I** *was hurt. By assigning reasons for my hurt, I had been blaming other people for my negative beliefs and emotions when I should have been taking* *responsibility for them. If I did not take responsibility for my negative thoughts and beliefs, there was nothing I could do to change my emotional well-being. He said that I had met the enemy and the enemy was me. The good news, he added, was that I could do something about myself. I couldn't change anyone else.*

During my counseling sessions, the first thing I typically do is to have the client run through the Chocolate or Vanilla exercise. The point is twofold: The first intent of the exercise is to drive home the point that **we are responsible for our own emotions and beliefs.** Shelly could have given me a long list of reasons for her hurt, but they would all be based on blaming someone else for who she was. She was the one who was hurt, and until she took responsibility for her hurt, there was nothing she could do to change her mind and her emotions.

Second, the client must see that **we can make a choice without having a reason. In other words, it is possible for us to choose to believe what God's Word says about us, rather than believing false**

**beliefs.** We could give a million reasons why we believe that our false beliefs are true, but the fact is, those beliefs are no longer true now that we are saved and forgiven. Despite the many reasons we might have for believing otherwise, we can choose God's truth.

## Taking Responsibility

> The man said, "The woman you put here with me—she gave me some fruit from the tree, and I ate it." Then the LORD God said to the woman, "What is this you have done?" The woman said, "The serpent deceived me, and I ate."
>
> -Genesis 3:12-13

Taking responsibility has been a challenge from the beginning. When Adam and Eve sinned, God came to them in the garden. Immediately Adam blamed Eve, and Eve blamed the serpent.[1] Neither was willing to take responsibility. Like Adam and Eve, we tend to blame others instead of taking responsibility for ourselves.

Blaming someone else, if taken to an extreme, ends in homicide. Blaming ourselves, if taken to an extreme, leads to suicide. Blame (condemnation) of any kind never leads down a productive path. Blaming is something we are all accustomed to doing. Instead, we must learn to separate our emotions and ourselves from the sins of others.

For example, in chapter 1, Elaine was initially blaming her daughter for the way she felt: the child **made** her angry. Elaine was not even aware that she was blaming. There was nothing Elaine could do to change the child. She needed to take responsibility for her own false beliefs, and change her mind about who she was in Christ. When she did take responsibility for her own flawed beliefs, she was able to change her mind about being insecure, and she began to discipline the child in love and with confidence. Once she did this, the child began to exhibit godly behavior.

We cannot change another person; we can only change ourselves through God's healing Word. Very often, however, a change in our behavior will affect the behavior of those around us.

Blaming others for our feelings and beliefs blocks our healing. We need to take responsibility for our own feelings and beliefs so that we can change our minds. You've heard people say, "It is what it is." In this case we must admit, "I am what I am." There is no need to condemn; it just requires acceptance so that we can take responsibility and initiate a change. We can change our minds about who we are. We can simply make the declaration of our choice, and when our minds believes the truth, we will find the freedom to let the lie go. (We will talk more about changing our minds and letting go of beliefs and thoughts in a later chapter).

*Brenda's Testimony*

*I had to pick up and carry my old beliefs to the cross. There I could leave them behind, and be transformed into what God says I am. To him, I am the daughter of the King. I am anointed for a purpose that is important in His kingdom. The difficult thing is, or was, that I had to **pick up those old beliefs**, and bring them to the cross. **I had to acknowledge that I had them.** They were my beliefs, and* *as Dr. Retherford always said, "You can't give away what you don't own." I think a lot of people try to avoid their negative thoughts, bury their feelings, and hope they will go away somehow. After all, we're told that Christians aren't supposed to have such feelings. Pretending the feelings and beliefs aren't there doesn't work. In fact, it only makes the emotions attached to the beliefs stronger the longer they are ignored.*

## Believing God

In addition to shirking her responsibility for her sin by blaming the devil, Eve's actions also illustrate a lack of trust in God. This is another pattern in our lives that keeps us from being free. Eve did not believe God when He said she would die if she ate from the Tree of the Knowledge of Good and Evil. She did not need to know all the facts to believe Him. She didn't have to have it all figured out; she just needed to believe God because He is God. Unfortunately, she did not believe God when He said that she would die.

Much of what keeps us from being healed emotionally comes from our doubting or outright disagreeing with God's Word about who we are and who He is. Doubting of God's Word can come from a lack of faith or sheer ignorance of what the Word says.

> *The mind governed by the flesh is hostile to God.*
>
> -Romans 8:7a

The Bible says that the carnal mind is hostile toward God.[2] If we are hostile toward God, we are not engaged in a trusting relationship with Him. The Word of God renews our minds, builds our faith, and draws us nearer to God.

Changing our minds to be in agreement with who God says we are requires an understanding of the scriptures. We need to know who we are in Christ. I suggest that clients working through this healing process spend a significant amount of time reading the Word every day.

I once had a client, who was a Vietnam veteran exhibiting horrible signs of fear and irrational behavior. He had nightmares on a regular basis, and even when he was awake, he believed that people were trying to kill him. He was so fear stricken that he wouldn't even go out in public. As we dealt head on with his irrational thoughts, he was able to let go of the fear and choose to believe the Word of God. The Word says not to worry about those who can kill the body; but to fear God who is in control of our salvation. Once this man gained a godly perspective and truly believed in his heart that God was protecting him, he was able to return to a more productive way of life. He didn't really have a reason for believing God's Word, but he chose to believe it anyway.

## **Endnotes**

[1] Gen. 3:12-13

[2] Rom. 8:7a

# CHAPTER 4

# <u>IDENTIFYING OUR FALSE BELIEFS</u>

After I review the Chocolate or Vanilla exercise with my clients, I move onto the next step. To help my clients identify their false beliefs, I present them with a list of words that describe some of the false beliefs of all human beings. This list represets who we were in our flesh or in our sin nature. The next page shows an example of a list I might use.

First, I have my clients read through the list slowly, stating each word in a sentence. For example, they might say, "I am doubtful," or "I am impatient," or "I am nervous." They should say it with as much meaning as possible to see whether they connect with the belief or whether there is any emotion attached to it. Some of these words seem more like emotions than beliefs but sometimes we allow these words to define who we are. For example, we say, "I am angry," as if it defines who we are, not how we feel.

I have the client continue through the entire list so that we can see which false beliefs hold an "emotional charge."

## List of False Beliefs

| Doubtful | Hateful | Abandoned |
|---|---|---|
| Impatient | Fearful | Unlovable |
| Nervous | Stupid | Undeserving |
| Sad | Guilty | Insignificant |
| Confused | Embarrassed | Meaningless |
| Grieved | Ashamed | Useless |
| Discouraged | Humiliated | Incapable |
| Powerless | Rejected | Incompetent |
| Abused | Envious | Not good enough |
| Bitter | Weak | Inadequate |
| Disappointed | Failure | Insufficient |
| Regretful | Insecure | Inferior |
| Offended | Helpless | Ugly |
| Resentful | Powerless | Rotten |
| Angry | Empty | Not OK |
| Hurt | Alone | Worthless |

The words that evoke pain when confessed represent the beliefs that are keeping the person in bondage to the past. I ask the clients to circle the beliefs or emotions that seem to be the biggest problems for them. When they can deal with these false beliefs and change their minds to be in line with God's Word, they will go free in Christ.

## Teresa's Story

Teresa came to me with many issues revolving around the guilt she had from the environment in which her children were raised. Her oldest daughter, Sharon, was particularly dysfunctional. When Sharon was a small child, Teresa had a terrible alcohol addiction. Sharon had been neglected at times and was exposed to things and people that a child should not be subjected to. Teresa, however, had received her freedom from her addiction when Sharon was young, and she had become a devout Christian with very active faith. She brought her children to church and cared for them to the best of her ability, given that she was a single mom with several mouths to feed.

Now Sharon was an adult with children of her own. She was addicted to crack, and this addiction impeded her from being a good mother to her children. Her children were constantly scattered from one home to the next as the grandparents and others tried to take care of them. Teresa was frequently rescuing Sharon from the results of Sharon's bad behavior. Teresa was operating out of guilt, and she felt it was her fault that Sharon was an addict.

I worked with Teresa through the same process that I use with all my clients. As we discussed in chapter 3, I first had her work through the Chocolate or Vanilla exercise. This taught her that **she could make a choice without a reason.** It also made her aware that **she was responsible for her beliefs and emotions**. She needed to give the sins of others to the Lord and focus strictly on her false beliefs.

Teresa was quick to catch on to the concept of dealing with her thoughts and beliefs, and not wasting time and energy discussing the sins of her children. She was bold and courageous about facing a number of false beliefs she had, the biggest of which was her belief that she was guilty. We identified her issue with guilt by using the list of false beliefs and the process I described earlier. I had her speak all the negative beliefs on the list so that we could identify the beliefs that were plaguing her the most. It was easy to see that she had a tremendous amount of negative emotion attached to the belief that she was guilty.

In her old nature, of course, she **was** guilty, as we all are. She had to accept this, and, with acceptance; came a tremendous amount of emotion. Guilt had been running and ruining her life. Jesus had died for the forgiveness of her sins, but she was unable to release her false belief that she was still guilty. She had to take responsibility for who she was in her sinful nature. In doing so she could experience and release the flood of emotions that came with the thought "I am guilty."

After releasing her emotions, she could clearly see she had been forgiven and she was a new creation in Christ. [1] Once free from the guilt that had haunted her for decades, she was able to establish healthier boundaries with her children. She no longer felt responsible for taking care of her adult children or rescuing them from their

> *Therefore, if anyone is in Christ, the new creation has come: The old has gone, the new is here!*
>
> **-2 Corinthians 5:17**

problems. Guilt was no longer in control, and most of her children's behavior improved with her new attitudes about where her responsibility stopped and where theirs began.

## Purification

After receiving salvation, God allows us to go through a purification process in order to expose emotions that block us from changing our mindsets and beliefs. This purification is part of our sanctification. Sanctification is the process of becoming holy. As our beliefs begin to line up with the truth (we are holy), our behavior begins to line up with God's will.

We all have flawed beliefs about who we are. Beneath these beliefs often lie very potent negative emotions that have built up in our souls. Very often, these emotions need to be released before we can experience the opportunity to change our minds and walk in the Spirit. God helps allow these emotions and beliefs to surface through the purification process. Our negative emotions are really just pain that is attached to our negative and false beliefs. We will never remove every bit of hurt and pain from our souls while we live in our present bodies, but we need to get to a point where our emotions don't control our actions, and we have room for the indwelling Spirit of God to overflow with love through us. As God allows us to be purified through the trials of our lives, our emotions can be released, making room for God's Holy Spirit to manifest itself fully through the fruits of the Spirit.

We tend to do three things when dealing with our emotions and false beliefs. Rather than accept them and take responsibility for them, (1) we resist – this manifests itself in arguments and fights; (2) we suppress – this means we just keep pushing our negative thoughts and feelings down; or (3) we avoid, – which shows up as an addiction. When we admit our false beliefs; and tell the truth as we believe it— "I am disappointed," or "I am unworthy," or "I am not good enough"—we can begin to take ownership of our false beliefs and negative emotions. Remember, these things were true when we were in our sin nature but they are no longer true now that we are in Christ. Coming to accept God's truth about who we are in Christ requires working through our emotions and eventually coming to a point where we can change our minds.

### Elizabeth's Testimony

During our first session, Dr. Retherford handed me a list of words that represent negative emotions or beliefs that a person might have (see appendix A). He asked me to start reading them out loud one at a time while inserting "I am" in front of each one. This was fine until I got midway down the page, and I came to the word "unlovable." Trying to confess "I am unlovable" was impossible for me to do through my tears. I was crying harder than I had in a long time. I had been through years of secular counseling, and I had never cried like this. This guy, in a matter of thirty minutes, had me crying so hard that I couldn't speak. I thought it was great that he had gotten to what seemed like the root of my emotions in such a short time. I would have to work through these emotions to be able to see God's truth about who I really was. I knew the Bible said that God loves me, but I had so much emotion about feeling unlovable that it was impossible for me to accept God's love at that time.

The process I have my patients follow to take ownership of their false beliefs is just what you would imagine. I have them sit in a chair, looking directly into my eyes. I have them speak their beliefs to me until their negative emotions are dispersed. For example, Elizabeth confessed, "I am unlovable," until her emotions were released and she was free to see clearly the truth that is explained in the gospel. The truth is; she is loved. God **is** love, and it is impossible for Him not to love her.

The surfacing of the sins of others during the process is normal, but the focus should remain on the false belief of the client. I often need to gently remind my clients of the Chocolate or Vanilla exercise and the fact that we need to let the sins of others go to God. Blaming others for our false beliefs will not result in healing. Blame or condemnation in any form is counterproductive. If the client struggles too much with the concept of not blaming, I may return to the Chocolate or Vanilla exercise described in chapter 3 to remind the person of how the healing process works.

Eventually, through the client's recognizing and

admitting the false belief, the emotion will subside and the client will be able to choose to believe what the Word of God says about him or her (see appendix B). We will talk more about making a choice without a reason in chapter 5.

Elizabeth was able to change her mind about being unlovable as soon as she dealt with her emotions attached to her false belief. She dealt with the emotion by admitting that she was "unlovable." Much like lancing a boil, once she opened the floodgates, all her negative emotion and grief poured out, clearing the way for her to change her mind and know that she was loved.

# **Endnotes**

[1] 2 Cor. 5:17

# CHAPTER 5

# CHANGING OUR MINDS TO GOD'S TRUTH

The concept of changing our minds is pivotal to the message of this book. With God's help we can change our minds through making a choice to believe the truth that is written in the scriptures. **God's Word defines who we are, and we need to accept His truth over our beliefs about who we were in our past.** We must take those false beliefs to the cross one by one and exchange them for the truth of God's Word. We make these choices by the grace of God.

Remember Elaine, the woman who was afraid to punish her daughter? She had to accept who she used to be and change her mind to be who God said she was. She believed that she was insecure and incompetent; however, the truth is that in Christ she is both secure and competent. She had to admit who she thought she was in her past, take those false beliefs to the cross, die to those beliefs, and choose to believe what the Word of God says about her. This process can be difficult and painful, but it is necessary for our walk with Christ and freedom in Him. We have to choose to make these changes in our mindset.

## Mary's Story

Mary consistently married men who were physically abusive to her. She had been married several times, and all her marriages ended because of abuse. She was concerned that she could not make a good decision about a future spouse because she didn't understand why she continued to make the same mistake. While working with Mary, I discovered that she had been abused as a child and held false beliefs about being unworthy and hurt. As we worked through her emotions by having her accept and admit her false beliefs, she was able to change her mind to line up with the truth according to the Word. She no longer believed she was hurt; she was healed and she was also worthy through Christ to have a godly relationship and marriage.

As with all my clients, I started by having Mary

run through the Chocolate or Vanilla exercise. During this exercise she learned that she could choose an ice cream without having any reason for choosing it. For example, she could choose chocolate simply because she chose chocolate. This helped her realize that she could admit that she felt unworthy because she felt unworthy. In other words, she accepted that she held the belief without blaming others, herself, or her circumstance. You've heard the phrase, "it is what it is." It's the same concept – she had to let go of the reasons and admit that it simply "is." She simply believed she was unworthy. This is an important concept to grasp in the process of choosing God's truth. If we get stuck in the many reasons why we have false beliefs, we may never change our minds to God's truth.

It is true that before we accepted Christ, we were all unworthy. Mary's life experiences of abuse certainly led her to believe that she was unworthy of being treated with the respect that every person deserves. If Mary were to base her beliefs on her past experiences, and all the many reasons she could give, she would most likely believe that she was unworthy. Simply considering what God's Word says, without looking at the reasons, would allow her to choose to believe that she is worthy of being treated as a child of God. Her husband should love and respect her just as Jesus loves and respects the church.

Once she understood the concepts taught in the Chocolate or Vanilla exercise, we were able to identify her false beliefs that had kept her bound. As always, we did this by reviewing the list of false beliefs (see appendix A). While reviewing the list, and speaking each word, she realized that she was emotionally stuck on being unworthy and hurt.

Having identified the major emotional stumbling blocks in her life, we had her speak these beliefs until the emotion had dissipated. At that point she could weigh the truth between whether she was unworthy or worthy.

Once we get to this point, we can exercise our free will to choose. For example, we can choose to believe we are worthy because of Christ, as Mary did, or we can choose to believe we are unworthy because of our pasts. We can choose to believe that we are who God says we are, or we can believe that we are who we used to be. **The choice is ours.** Mary chose to be worthy through the blood of Jesus and her life changed dramatically because of it.

## Changing Our Minds

To change our minds, we have to know what the Word of God says about who we are when we are born again into Christ (see appendix B). We have to understand that once we are born again into Christ, we are new creations in Him,[1] deserving of all the benefits and promises from God that come with being a child of the King. We are not worthy of these things through anything we have done; it is only through Christ that we are righteous and deserving.[2]

Most of us must take our ungodly beliefs one by one to the cross, leave them there, and change our minds to His truth. Taking our beliefs to the cross means we must accept who we were in our sinful nature. The new revelation of who we are in Christ usually comes as head knowledge first before it is truly accepted in our hearts. Once we believe it in our heads and we continue to decree its truth, we will receive the revelation and believe it in our hearts. We will talk more about decreeing in chapter 6.

Once we have experienced the changing of our minds to God's truth, we will also see a change in our characters, as our beliefs define who we are.

In the earlier examples of healing that I've described, my clients all received breakthroughs in their healing process by changing their minds to believe God's Word. You can review a summary of their choices and the victories they experienced in the chart on the next page.

For example, if the Word of God says we are accepted, we need to change our minds about being rejected. Maybe we've been rejected all our lives. We believe we're rejected because we have been rejected. However, we are not rejected anymore, and to believe that we are rejected is to call God a liar. We are accepted in Him no matter what we have done or where we have come from.

| Presenting problem | False belief | Biblical belief | Outcome |
|---|---|---|---|
| Misbehaving child | Insecure and incompetent as a mother | Secure and competent in Christ | Disciplined out of godly love and child is well behaved |
| Vietnam veteran with irrational fear and behavior | Fear of man | God is in control and we are safe in Him | Able to leave house and live a more productive life |
| Husband was cheating on her | Anger, unforgiveness and hurt | Forgiveness, love sinners where they are | Husband came back and sought counseling |
| Adult child running her life | Guilt | Forgiven through Christ and child is responsible for herself | Freedom from adult child's bad behavior |
| Several abusive marriages | Unworthy | Worthy and deserving of godly relationships | Moved forward with a stable and normal lifestyle |

Some might be wondering how it is possible to change our minds to a belief that is contrary to everything that our pasts have taught us. It's simple: you **choose** to do it. In my sessions I distinguish between choices and decisions. Decisions always have reasons and for the purposes of our work in counseling, **choices don't have reasons**. I always use the following two examples when I am conducting workshops. The first is an example of a decision.

I saw a movie once in which a young man was driving down the road and a person cut him off. The young man started to curse and swear at the other driver. He was very angry at the man who had cut him off. The young man's grandfather was sitting next to him and asked him whether the person who had cut him off was responsible for the boy's thoughts and feelings. When we have reasons outside ourselves for our emotions and beliefs, we are always helpless to the effects of our circumstances. The young man was blaming the other driver for his anger. To me, this is an example of a decision because a reason was given—the boy had been cut off, and that person "**made** him angry."

Here is what I consider to be a choice. Remember, we can make a choice without having a reason. I went to my neighbor and asked him whether I could borrow his shovel. The neighbor said; "no." I asked him why he had said no, and he said, "If I am not going to lend you the shovel, I am not going to lend you the shovel." Where choice is concerned, "what is, is." This man did not offer a reason, he simply chose not to lend me his shovel. Likewise, we can simply **choose** to change our minds for no reason at all. We are in control of our thoughts. We should not allow others and our circumstances to have power over us. Only God should have such power in our lives.

We can change our minds by making a choice regardless of what our pasts have taught us. God can make choices without reasons. God said to Moses, "I will have mercy on whom I have mercy, and I will have compassion on whom I have compassion."[3] As I always tell my clients when they are making a choice, "What is, is." There does not have to be a reason, just as God has mercy because He has mercy, we can choose to believe it because we choose to believe it.

If we can't choose to believe that we are accepted, it is probably because there is a lot of emotion tied up in the beliefs that we are rejected. It is also possible that we are still blaming people or circumstances for our false belief. God desires for us to believe His Word and to believe that we are accepted.

*Lynn's Testimony*

*I had been sexually abused as a child, and I always felt abandoned by God. Why did He allow those things to happen to me? Dr. Retherford had continually stressed that I could change my mind about those false beliefs and negative emotions on that list (see Appendix A). I was finally beginning to get the breakthrough. After a time of walking with God through the trials and tribulations, I was able to accept the fact that I am not abandoned. I always believed I was abandoned. I projected all my childhood abandonment onto God. Anytime anything went wrong it stirred up that belief and I would rage and shout at the Lord. I'm surprised He didn't strike me dead. I mean, I said some really awful things. I vacillated between blaming God, blaming my perpetrator, and blaming myself when all I had to do was take responsibility for my false belief and change my mind. I was able to change my mind. I am not abandoned. In fact, I never was abandoned. God has always been with me, and I know that He protected me from even greater harm that could have come if He had not been with me.*

Very often my clients will tell me, "I'm *trying* to change my mind." When people tell me they are *trying* to make a choice to change their minds, I often show them the following exercise to make a point.

I will ask the person to try to stand up. Most of us don't even think about standing up, we just do it. When I ask someone to try to stand up he or she doesn't understand what I am asking. How can a person try to stand up without actually doing it? Changing one's mind once the emotion is gone is like standing up; you just do it.

If clients cannot change their minds it is possible that they have not fully accepted the truth about their false beliefs. For example, if people believe they are unworthy, they have to be fully accepting of the fact that they **were** unworthy before they were saved. Once we admit who we were, we will be able to change our minds to God's truth.

As we work through our emotions, we can ask the Holy Spirit for His help and guidance to change our minds to be in agreement with God's Word.

Ultimately, it is up to us to make the choice.

Remember, we can make a choice without a reason.

A story in the Gospel of Luke shows how Peter received a breakthrough by making a choice to believe Christ. Peter had been out fishing all night and had not caught anything. If you have ever gone fishing, you know that after a few hours of not catching a fish you are ready to call it quits. Despite the reasons Peter had to disbelieve Jesus, Peter chose to believe Jesus and do what He said to do.

> *Simon answered, "Master, we've worked hard all night and haven't caught anything. But because you say so, I will let down the nets."*
>
> -Luke 5:4-6

Jesus said to Peter, "Put out into deep water and let down the nets for a catch." Peter replied, "Master, we've worked hard all night and haven't caught anything, but because you say so, I will let down the nets."[4] Peter first gave Jesus a reason for not believing Him, but then Peter made the critical choice to believe Jesus without having a reason. As a result of

Peter's choice made without a reason, they caught so many fish that two boats full of fish were beginning to sink. After this first experience in choosing to believe God without a reason, Peter worshiped Jesus and left everything he owned to follow Jesus and become His disciple.

This is the type of experience we are likely to have when we press through to receive our first breakthrough. We need to follow the process, trust the Lord, study our Word and believe the Holy Spirit will assist us in making this first critical choice to believe His Word rather than our old false belief. We must be persistent and continue to admit our false belief to God until we are ready to make a choice. From time to time, we should ask ourselves, "Am I willing to change my mind?" If the answer is "no," we must press through until the change comes. Once it comes, we will see that God opens up a whole new level of faith. Further breakthrough will become easier and easier.

## Endnotes

[1] 2 Cor. 5:17

[2] Rom. 9:30, Eph. 4:24, Phil. 3:9

[3] Rom. 9:15

[4] Luke 5:4-6

# CHAPTER 6

# <u>PUTTING ON THE NEW MAN</u>

We are saved by grace through faith.[1] We did not obtain our spiritual identities through anything we have done. They come only through our belief that God has changed us into the truth reflected in His Word. There is nothing we can do to be good enough in His eyes except to believe that His son died for us and rose from the dead. Through Jesus's sacrifice, we are dead to sin and alive to the Spirit. All we have to do is choose to believe.

> *For it is by grace you have been saved, through faith – and this is not from yourselves, it is the gift of God – not by works so that no one can boast.*
>
> -Ephesians 2:8-9

Grace can also help us to realize what faith has already done. In other words, when our faith causes us to believe God's Word, by grace we can change our minds. Jesus said, God's Word is truth. He asked God to sanctify us by that truth.[2] The truth of His Word has the power to make us holy. We must get the truth of His Word into our mind and subsequently rooted in our heart. Then our actions will begin to line up with the will of God and we will live in a more holy manner.

I believe that Christians desire to walk in love. It is impossible, however, for us to override our false beliefs and walk in love through our willpower. Paul, in his letter to the Colossians, explained that we are to "put on the new self, which is

> *Put on the new self, which is being renewed in knowledge in the image of its Creator.*
>
> -Colossians 3:10

being renewed in knowledge in the image of its Creator."[3] The new self is who we are according to God. In God's eyes we are holy and are made in His image. It is this image, the image of Christ, that we are to "put on." Paul goes on to say that over all the virtues of God, we are to put on love.[4] When we put on the image of God we are walking in the Spirit of God, allowing God's love to flow through us in abundance. This supernatural transformation comes only through faith and our ability to let go of false beliefs and choose to believe the Word of God.

The fact that Paul instructs us to put off the old and put on the new suggests that we have something we have to do. "Put off" and "put on" on are action words. What actions must we take to do what Paul is asking us to do?

## The Power of the Word

To put on the new man, we must know and use the Word of God. The Word of God is supernatural. It leads to healing and revelation that is not possible through earthly means. The gospel (the good news about Jesus Christ) is the power of God.

The Bible tells us who we are when we are born into Christ. It tells us what Jesus did for us at Calvary so we could be set free. Our old selves died with Him on the cross, and we are now reborn into Christ. God says we are heirs and co-heirs with Christ.[5] This is what makes us deserving of God's promises, protection, and blessings.

When Christ ascended to be with the Father, He sent His Holy Spirit to help teach us and bring revelation to us. He also left the words that He taught. John tells us that Jesus "was the Word."[6] The writer of the book of Hebrews tells us, "The Son is the radiance of God's glory and the exact representation of his being sustaining all things by his **powerful word**."[7] Imagine how much power the Word has! It is capable of

> *In the beginning was the Word, and the Word was with God, and the Word was God. He was with God in the beginning.*
>
> -John 1:1-2

sustaining (maintaining) everything in the entire universe. There is such power in the Word of God, and that same power that Christ exhibited on earth is now present here through His Word and the Holy Spirit. The Word and the Holy Spirit have the power to renew our minds. This is why it is so important that we seek God's wisdom and healing power through His Word.

First, we must read and understand God's Word. We have been supernaturally recreated into the truth represented in the gospel of Jesus Christ. We no longer have to make our choices based on our pasts, what man thinks, or even our own thoughts. We believe the Word of God and are free from false beliefs that pervert our thinking and cause us to act out of our flesh rather than walking in the Spirit of God. With God's help, we can transform our thinking to be in line with the Spirit of God rather than the flesh and the world. It is through this transformation that we can now put on the Spirit of God and all the fruit of that Spirit.

The next practical step we can take is to force ourselves to think what the Word of God says. In other words, we can force ourselves to have thoughts such as, "I am a loving person. I am a kind person, I am the righteousness of God in Christ." We can go about telling ourselves these truths all day long. If clients are dealing with false beliefs, have them identify a scripture that brings God's truth to the situation. Have them think about this scripture every time they have a negative thought or emotional reaction to a false belief. It is amazing how quickly their beliefs will line up with their thoughts. Once their beliefs line up with their thoughts, which are the Word of God, then their behavior will begin to line up with the will of God.

Romans says, "Don't copy the behavior and customs of this world, but let God transform you into a new person **by changing the way you think.**" [8] If you truly believe the Word of God, it won't matter what the world is telling you, you can choose to change your mind. The Bible also says, "Those who are dominated by the sinful nature think about sinful things, but those who are controlled by the Holy Spirit think about things that please the Spirit."[9] It is amazing how quickly our beliefs will line up with our thoughts as we begin to force our mind to think what the scriptures say.

Another way to seal the transition of putting on the new man is to make decrees about who we are in

Christ - for example, "I am loving; I am kind; I am patient" (see appendix B). The Bible says, "Thou shalt also decree a thing, and it shall be established unto thee: and the light shall shine upon thy ways."[10] We put on the new man by decreeing who we are in Christ. Most of us are familiar with this process. The power is in the tongue. The bible says, "The tongue has power of life and death."[11]

The word "decree" is actually a legal term meaning "an official ruling or law. God's decree is His settled plan and purpose."[12] When we decree something from the Word of God, we are making it legally binding in a spiritual sense. There is power in our tongues and there is creative power in the decreeing of God's Word.

The Word of God is absolute truth, and by speaking it through faith, we legislate a change in our hearts, our minds, and our lives. Again, have clients identify a scripture dealing with their false beliefs. Have them begin to decree its truth over their lives.

God has given us the power to change our circumstances through the words of our mouths. Our tongues have creative power to make change if we speak spiritual truths into our lives. Remember that the

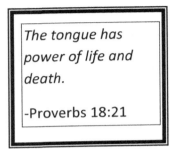

*The tongue has power of life and death.*

-Proverbs 18:21

purpose of the Chocolate or Vanilla process is to go free in Christ. We must know that God has filled us with the fruit of His Spirit and decree that we are loving, peaceful, gentle, and kind.

This is not to say that we have arrived and are perfect, but we could say that we have arrived at a major breakthrough in our lives and our walk with Jesus. We are in a place where we have a process to follow to change our minds and turn back to God if we fall into negative thinking.

## Keeping Our Freedom

Usually, things that happen throughout a day are trivial and can be dealt with in a matter of minutes or even seconds. The key is dealing with the negative emotions and thoughts quickly. We should practice immediate forgiveness and we should change our minds quickly. After we change our minds, we decree the positive. Sometimes decreeing the Word of God can help us to change our minds.

Believing God's Word, changing our thoughts and decreeing God's Word over our lives are some steps to "putting on" the Spirit. "Thank you Lord that I am patient. Thank you Lord that I am kind. Thank you that I am seated in heavenly places with Christ. I am a new creation in Christ."[13] Force yourself to meditate on the scriptures and decree the scriptures out loud.

We are now in a place where emotions should no longer keep us bound. We can separate people from their sin and daily put off the old man and put on the new. The Word says, "Where the Spirit of the Lord is there is freedom."[14] As circumstances arise, if we begin to get a negative attitude, we can take a thirty-second time-out and get rid of the old and put on the new. Changing our minds in regard to trivial issues will be quick for us at this point. We can find a place of solitude and work through our emotions. We literally pray the scriptures and plead the blood of Jesus over our thought lives. We can take control, and with the help of the Holy Spirit, we can change our disposition.

On a bad day, we may need to take several hours to pray and get our attitudes renewed. Sometimes life circumstances require a deeper healing, and it may take months to get healed and let go of wrong thinking. The acceptance of false beliefs and the releasing of emotions will likely be necessary. Don't get discouraged if this type of healing experience should arise after you have learned to walk in the Spirit. Healing is a process, and there will always be things that we need to deal with. The difference is now we have a process to work through to get back to the love and freedom of Christ.

## **Endnotes**

[1] Eph. 2:8-9

[2] John 17:17

[3] Col. 3:10

[4] Col. 3:14a

[5] Rom 8:17

[6] John 1:1-2

[7] Heb. 1:3a, emphasis added

[8] Rom. 12:2, (NLT), emphasis added

[9] Rom 8:5, (NLT)

[10] Job 22:28, (KJV)

[11] Prov. 18:21a

[12] Merrill C. Tenney and J.D. Douglas, *New International Bible Dictionary: Based on the NIV* (Grand Rapids, MI: Zondervan Pub. House, 1987)

[13] Gal. 5:22-23, Eph. 2:6, 2 Cor. 5:17

[14] 2 Cor. 3:17

# CHAPTER 7

# <u>SUMMARY OF THE PROCESS</u>

## Laying the Groundwork

God confers His righteousness to us. [1] Perhaps the most important thing for clients to accept and choose to believe is that they are righteous. Out of that righteousness comes much of their identities in Christ as shown in appendix B. They must whole heartedly understand that this righteousness is not earned. If it were earned, it could be taken away. They need to understand about God's grace and that they were made holy through what Christ did, not because of anything they did. If they don't understand this basic principle, take some time

> *Not having a righteousness of my own that comes from the law, but that which is through faith in Christ—the righteousness that comes from God on the basis of faith.*
>
> *-Philippians 3:9*

to work with them so they can get a better understanding of what it means to be saved by grace through faith. [2]

Review appendix B with them so that they can understand what God's Word says about them. This will become head knowledge to them but will lay a foundation for changing their minds in the future. The Word is the truth that they will be changing their minds to be in alignment with.

## Choice verses Decision

They must understand that **they can make a choice to change their minds without a reason.** They must understand this to succeed in going free. I use the Chocolate or Vanilla exercise described in chapter 3 with my clients as one of the first orders of business. This helps them to see how they can make a choice without a reason. It also shows them that they are responsible for their emotions. They need to focus on their own false beliefs and let the sins of others go to God.

The Chocolate or Vanilla exercise also helps clients stop blaming other people, circumstances, or themselves for their false beliefs. "Blame" is another word for "condemnation", and it is not what God desires.[3] They need to take responsibility for their thoughts without condemning themselves and others.

## Identify Their Thoughts and Beliefs

Next, I have clients speak the words on the list in appendix A with as much meaning as they can. They should insert the words "I am" before every word - for example, "I am unlovable." Some of these beliefs will have strong emotions attached to them. These emotions keep your clients blinded to the truth of who they are in Christ. Allow the emotion to come up as they read the list and have them release the emotion in the best way that they can.

Next, identify the one or two words that seem to have the greatest power over them emotionally. These are the words they should work on over the next few weeks. Have them identify at least one Bible verse that contradicts what they are feeling and believing so that they can meditate on it. They can also begin to decree these verses over their lives.

## Releasing Emotions

It is difficult for them to change their minds when they are overwhelmed by emotions that are attached to their negative and false beliefs. Feel free to have them repeat their false beliefs out loud to you as many times as necessary to get the emotion out. For example, they could say to you, "I am alone." I know it's not the truth but it's what they believe and the emotion attached to this lie is keeping them bound. They must release all the emotions that are connected to their negative beliefs as they work through the list shown in appendix A.

## Changing Their Minds

Admitting the false beliefs will bring them to a point where they can accept that this was who they were apart from God. Once they release the emotion, they should be able to change their mind. Attack one false belief at a time. When they are able to change their mind to be in agreement with God's truth, move onto the next false belief.

## Putting On Christ

Putting on the new man begins with whole heartedly believing the Word of God. For clients to believe the Word of God they must be reading the Word of God daily.

They can also choose to change their thoughts by taking scriptures in the Bible that fight against their negative beliefs and repeating those scriptures to themselves as they go about their day.

> *But the fruit of the Spirit is love, joy, peace, forbearance, kindness, goodness, faithfulness, gentleness and self-control.*
>
> **-Galatians 5:22-23**

Lastly, they can decree who they are in Christ (see appendix B). They can decree the fruit of the Spirit over their lives. The Bible says, "But the fruit of the Spirit is love, joy, peace, forbearance, kindness, goodness, faithfulness, gentleness and self-control. Against such things there is no law."[4] There are many other scriptures they can use to decree truth over their life. Allow the Holy Spirit to show them the best scriptures to use.

### Rejoice

When the breakthrough comes, celebrate by giving God the glory for their newfound freedom!

## <u>Endnotes</u>

[1] Phil 3:9

[2] Eph. 2:8

[3] Rom 8:1a

[4] Gal. 5:22-23

# APPENDIX A

# TABLE OF FALSE BELIEFS

| | | |
|---|---|---|
| Doubtful | Hateful | Abandoned |
| Impatient | Fearful | Unlovable |
| Nervous | Stupid | Undeserving |
| Sad | Guilty | Insignificant |
| Confused | Embarrassed | Meaningless |
| Grieved | Ashamed | Useless |
| Discouraged | Humiliated | Incapable |
| Powerless | Rejected | Incompetent |
| Abused | Envious | Not good enough |
| Bitter | Weak | Inadequate |
| Disappointed | Failure | Insufficient |
| Regretful | Insecure | Inferior |
| Offended | Helpless | Ugly |
| Resentful | Powerless | Rotten |
| Angry | Empty | Not OK |
| Hurt | Alone | Worthless |

# APPENDIX B

# DECREEING GOD'S WORD

## I am...

God's child (John 1:12)
Forgiven (Eph. 1:7)
A new creation (2 Cor. 5:17)
A temple of the Holy Spirit (1 Cor. 6:19)
Delivered from the power of darkness (Col. 1:13)
Blessed (Gal. 3:9)
Holy and without blame (1 Pet. 1:16)
Victorious (Rev. 21:7)
Set free (John 8:31-33)
Strong in the Lord (Eph. 6:10)
More than a conqueror (Rom 8:37)
In Christ (1 Cor. 1:30)
Accepted in the beloved (Rom. 15:7)
Complete in Him (Col. 2:10)
Free from condemnation (Rom 8:1)
Reconciled to God (2 Cor. 5:18)
In the world as He is in heaven (1 John 4:17)
Overtaken with blessings (Eph. 1:3)
The righteousness of God (2 Cor. 5:21)
Called of God (2 Tim. 1:9-11)
Chosen (1 Pet. 2:5)
Healed by the stripes of Jesus (1 Pet. 2:24)
Seated in heavenly places (Eph. 2:6)
Beloved of God (Col. 3:12)

# DECREEING GOD'S LOVE & THE FRUIT OF GOD'S SPIRIT

You can decree God's love and the fruit of His Spirit over your life by decreeing the following list of spiritual truths. You can also change your beliefs by beginning to think these things as you go through the day. These truths come from 1 Corinthians 13:4-7, which defines what love is. It also includes a list of the fruit of the Spirit as defined in Galatians 5:22-23. This is who you are in the Spirit. Choose to believe it!

| I am patient | I trust |
|---|---|
| I am kind | I hope |
| I do not envy | I persevere |
| I do not boast | I am loving |
| I am not puffed-up | I am joyful |
| I do not dishonor others | I am peaceful |
| I am not self-seeking | I am kind |
| I am not easily angered | I am good |
| I keep no record of wrongs | I am faithful |
| I do not delight in evil | I am gentle |
| I rejoice with the truth | I have self-control |

Made in United States
Orlando, FL
06 April 2023

31855365R00055